RHYTHM
Fundamental Studies in Rhythmic Counting
By
FRED BUGBEE

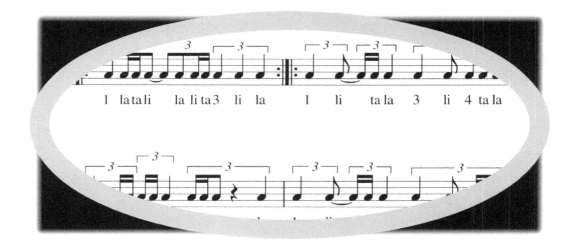

For additional material or additional copies, please visit us on the web at *www.fredbugbee.com*

Dedicated to:

Jerry Jr., Rick and Mary

CONTENTS

INSTRUCTIONS

The book is a graduated approach to learning rhythmic counting utilizing the Eastman System of Counting. The first line of each exercise should be viewed as a key and practiced individually until proficiency is achieved. The remaining three lines of each unit combine the initial exercises into a rhythmic etude.

Below are several principles to keep in mind regarding the system.

Notes beginning on the beat are called by the number of the beat.

When counting asymmetrical measures and compound meters, counting will depend on the unit of time getting the beat.

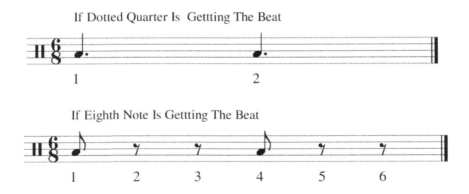

The syllable te (pronounced *tay*) is used for notes that are halfway between two beats.

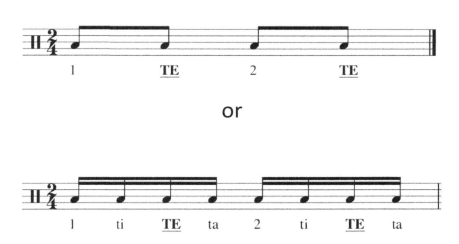

or

The syllable ti (pronounced *tee*) is used for notes beginning on the second 16th note of a beat.

The syllable ta (pronounced *tah*) is used for notes beginning on the last 16th note of a beat (Ta will also be used to fill in other rhythms, as will be demonstrated later).

The syllable la (pronounced *lah*) is used for notes beginning on the second third of a beat.

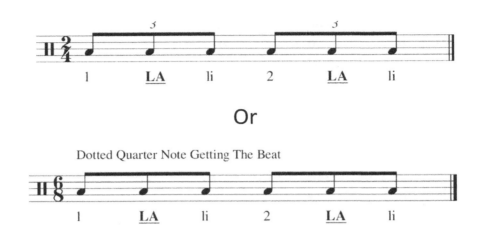

Or

Dotted Quarter Note Getting The Beat

The syllable li (pronounced *lee*) is used for notes beginning on the last third of a beat.

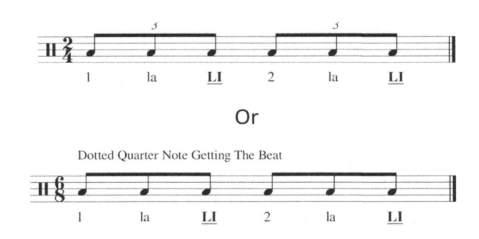

Or

Dotted Quarter Note Getting The Beat

The syllable ta is also used to count sextuplet figures, filling in the partials between the triplet.

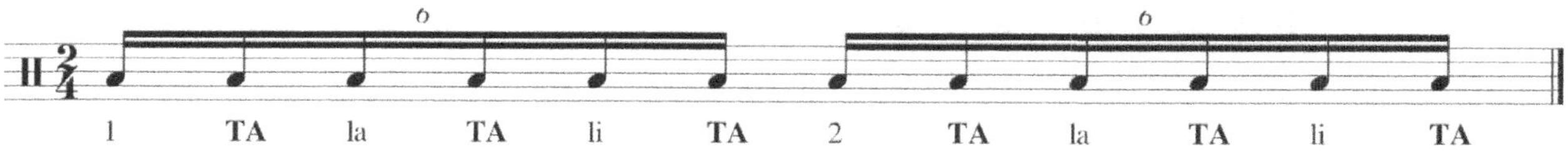

If a duple pulse is being emphasized as opposed to the triple pulse, the syllable te may be used on the fourth partial of the sextuplet.

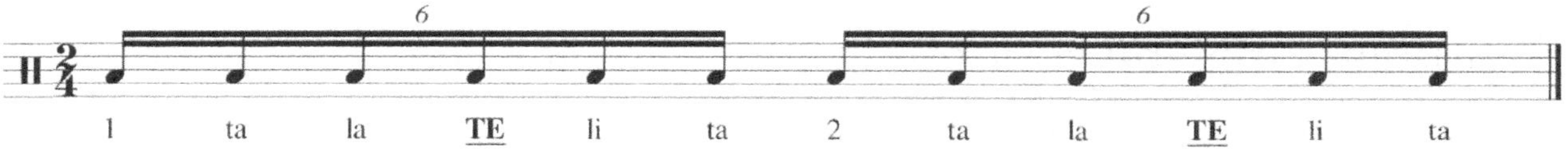

Or

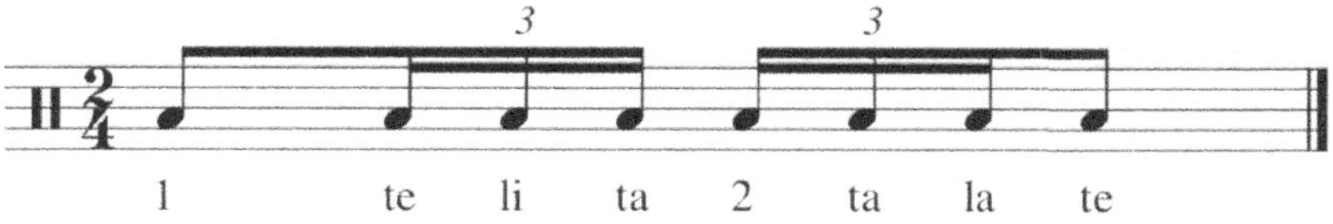

Ta is also used to fill in partials for 32nd note figures.

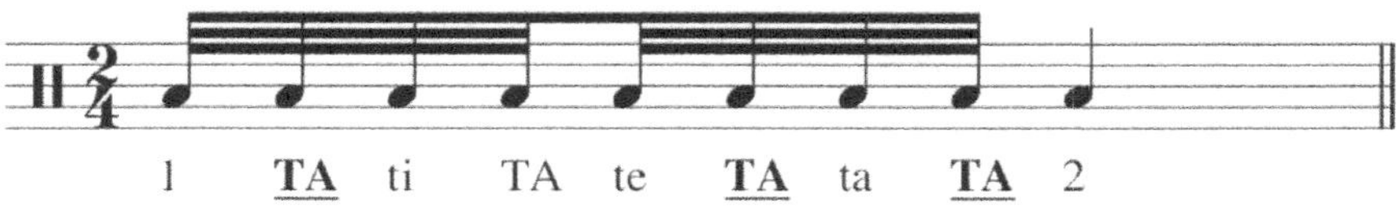

Quintuplets may be counted in the following manner (note that this is a deviation from the Eastman method).

The syllable ka (pronounced *kah*) is used for the second portion of a quintuplet. The syllable di (pronounced *dee*) is used for the third portion of a quintuplet. The syllable mi (pronounced *mee*) is used for the fourth portion of a quintuplet. The syllable ta (pronounced *tah*) is used for the fifth portion of a quintuplet.

Septuplets may be counted in the following manner (again, note that this is a deviation from the Eastman method).

Pronunciations are the same as noted above for quintuplets. The third and fifth note of the grouping share a syllable, as do the fourth and sixth.

SYLLABLE PRONUNCIATION GUIDE

Ti = Tee

Te = Tay

Ta = Tah

La = Lah

Li = Lee

Ka=Kah

Di=Dee

Mi=Mee

LESSON 1 – QUARTER NOTES AND HALF NOTES

1.

2.

3.

4.

5.

6.

3

9.

10.

5

11.

12.

13.

14.

LESSON 2 – EIGHTH NOTES

15.

16.

8

17.

1   2   te   3   4   1   te   2   3   4   te   1   2   te   3   te   4

1   te   2   3   4   te   1   2   te   3   4   1   2   te   3   te   4

1   2   te   3   te   4   1   te   2   3   4   te   1   2   te   3   4

1   2   te   3   4   1   2   te   3   te   4   1   te   2   3   4   te

18.

1   2   te   3   4   5   te   1   te   2   4   5   1   2   3   te   4   5

1   te   2   4   5   1   2   te   3   4   5   te   1   2   3   te   4   5

1   2   3   te   4   5   1   te   2   4   5   1   2   te   3   4   5   te

1   2   te   3   4   5   te   1   2   3   te   4   5   1   te   2   4   5

19.

20.

LESSON 3 – EIGHTH NOTE RESTS

21.

22.

23.

24.

25.

26.

27.

28.

29.

30.

LESSON 4 – SIXTEENTH NOTES

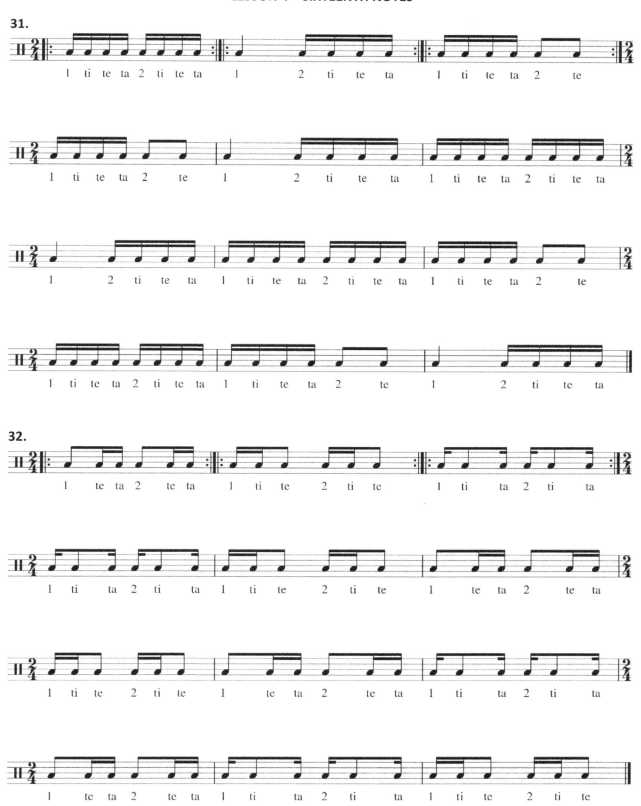

33.

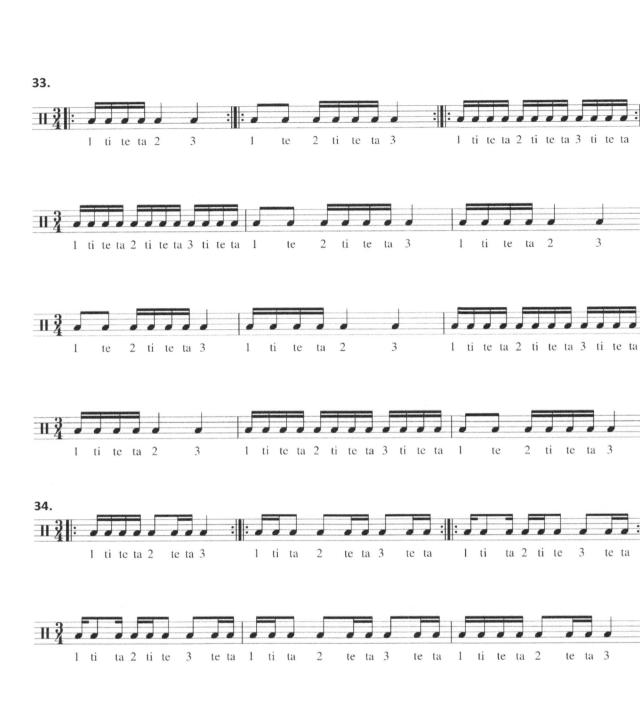

34.

35.

1 ti te ta 2   3 ti te ta 4 ti te ta   1   2 ti te ta 3 ti te ta 4 ti ta   1 ti te ta 2 te 3 ti te ta 4

1 ti te ta 2   3 ti te ta 4 ti te ta 1 ti te ta 2 te 3 ti te ta 4   1   2 ti te ta 3 ti te ta 4 ti ta

1 ti te ta 2 te 3 ti te ta 4   1   2 ti te ta 3 ti te ta 4 ti ta 1 ti te ta 2   3 ti te ta 4 ti te ta

1   2 ti te ta 3 ti te ta 4 ti ta 1 ti te ta 2   3 ti te ta 4 ti te ta 1 ti te ta 2 te 3 ti te ta 4

36.

1 te ta 2 te ta 3 ti te ta 4 te ta   1 ti te 2 ti te 3 te ta 4 ti ta   1 ti ta 2 ti te 3 te ta 4 ti te ta

1 te ta 2 te ta 3 ti te ta 4 te ta 1 ti ta 2 ti te 3 te ta 4 ti te ta 1 ti te 2 ti te 3 te ta 4 ti ta

1 ti ta 2 ti te 3 te ta 4 ti te ta 1 ti te 2 ti te 3 te ta 4 ti ta 1 te ta 2 te ta 3 ti te ta 4 te ta

1 ti te 2 ti te 3 te ta 4 ti ta 1 te ta 2 te ta 3 ti te ta 4 te ta 1 ti ta 2 ti te 3 te ta 4 ti te ta

37.

1 ti te ta 2 te 3 ti te ta 4 te ta 5 ti te ta   1 te ta 2 ti te ta 3 te 4 te ta 5 ti te ta   1 ti te 2 ti te ta 3 te 4 ti te ta 5 ti te

1 ti te 2 ti te ta 3 te 4 ti te ta 5 ti te   1 te ta 2 ti te ta 3 te 4 te ta 5 ti te ta   1 ti te ta 2 te 3 ti te ta 4 te ta 5 ti te ta

1 te ta 2 ti te ta 3 te 4 te ta 5 ti te ta   1 ti te ta 2 te 3 ti te ta 4 te ta 5 ti te ta   1 ti te 2 ti te ta 3 te 4 ti te ta 5 ti te

1 ti te ta 2 te 3 ti te ta 4 te ta 5 ti te ta   1 ti te 2 ti te ta 3 te 4 ti te ta 5 ti te   1 te ta 2 ti te ta 3 te 4 te ta 5 ti te ta

38.

1 ti te ta 2   3 ti te 4 te 5   6 ti te ta   1 te ta 2   3 ti te 4 te 5 ti te ta 6 te   1 ti te 2 te ta 3 te 4   5 te ta 6 ti te

1 ti te ta 2   3 ti te 4 te 5   6 ti te ta   1 ti te 2 te ta 3 te 4   5 te ta 6 ti te   1 te ta 2   3 ti te 4 te 5 ti te ta 6 te

1 ti te 2 te ta 3 te 4   5 te ta 6 ti te   1 te ta 2   3 ti te 4 te 5 ti te ta 6 te   1 ti te ta 2   3 ti te 4 te 5   6 ti te ta

1 te ta 2   3 ti te 4 te 5 ti te ta 6 te   1 ti te ta 2   3 ti te 4 te 5   6 ti te ta   1 ti te 2 te ta 3 te 4   5 te ta 6 ti te

39.

40.

41.

42.

45.

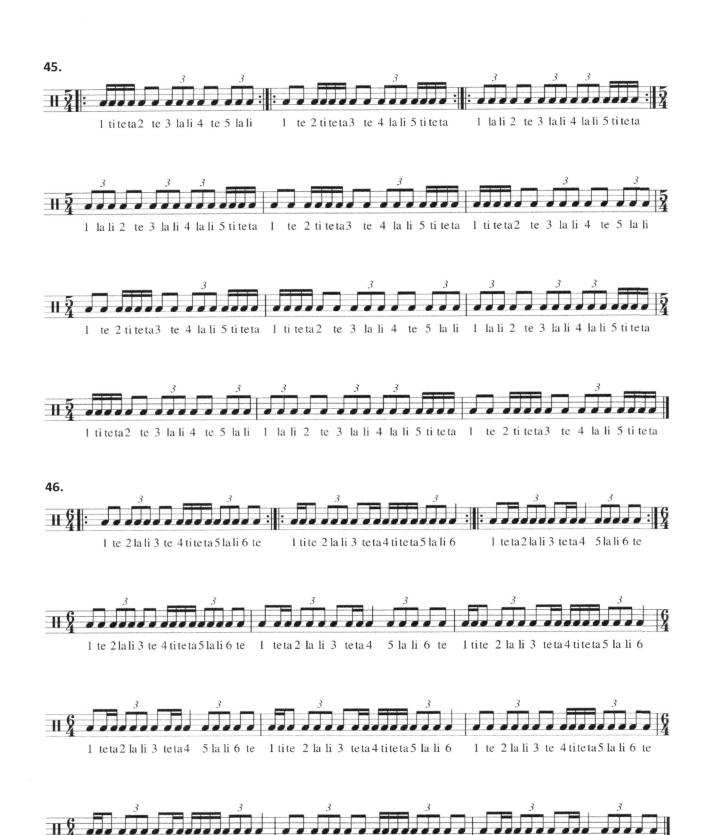

1 ti te ta 2 te 3 la li 4 te 5 la li   1 te 2 ti te ta 3 te 4 la li 5 ti te ta   1 la li 2 te 3 la li 4 la li 5 ti te ta

1 la li 2 te 3 la li 4 la li 5 ti te ta   1 te 2 ti te ta 3 te 4 la li 5 ti te ta   1 ti te ta 2 te 3 la li 4 te 5 la li

1 te 2 ti te ta 3 te 4 la li 5 ti te ta   1 ti te ta 2 te 3 la li 4 te 5 la li   1 la li 2 te 3 la li 4 la li 5 ti te ta

1 ti te ta 2 te 3 la li 4 te 5 la li   1 la li 2 te 3 la li 4 la li 5 ti te ta   1 te 2 ti te ta 3 te 4 la li 5 ti te ta

46.

1 te 2 la li 3 te 4 ti te ta 5 la li 6 te   1 ti te 2 la li 3 te ta 4 ti te ta 5 la li 6   1 te ta 2 la li 3 te ta 4   5 la li 6 te

1 te 2 la li 3 te 4 ti te ta 5 la li 6 te   1 te ta 2 la li 3 te ta 4   5 la li 6 te   1 ti te 2 la li 3 te ta 4 ti te ta 5 la li 6

1 te ta 2 la li 3 te ta 4   5 la li 6 te   1 ti te 2 la li 3 te ta 4 ti te ta 5 la li 6   1 te 2 la li 3 te 4 ti te ta 5 la li 6 te

1 ti te 2 la li 3 te ta 4 ti te ta 5 la li 6   1 te 2 la li 3 te 4 ti te ta 5 la li 6 te   1 te ta 2 la li 3 te ta 4   5 la li 6 te

LESSON 6 – DOTTED NOTES

24

49.

50.

53.

54.

55.

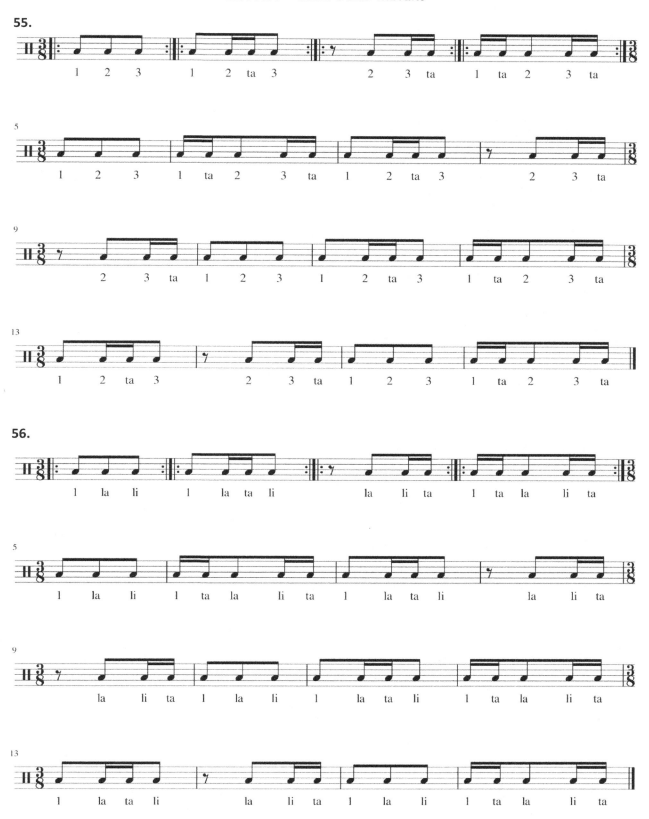

56.

57.

58.

29

59.

60.

61.

62.

63.

64.

32

65.

1   3 4   ten el tw   1 2   6 7 8   2   4   6   8   10   tw

1 2   6 7 8   2   4   6   8   10   tw 1   3 4   ten el tw

2   4   6   8   10   tw 1 2   6 7 8   1   3 4   ten el tw

1   3 4   ten el tw   2   4   6   8   10   tw 1 2   6 7 8

66.

1 li 2   la li   1 la li 2 li 3 la   li   1   li   la   3   li   la

1 la li 2 li 3 la   li 1   li   la   3   li   la 1   li 2   la li

1   li   la   3   li   la   1 la li 2 li 3 la   li 1   li 2   la li

1   li 2   la li 1   li   la   3   li   la   1 la li 2 li 3 la   li

67.

68.

69.

70.

73.

74.

75.

76.

77.

79.

80.

81.

1 2 3 4 5 6 7   1   3 4   6   1 2 3   5   7   1 2   4   6

1 2   4   6   1 2 3   5   7   1   3 4   6   1 2 3 4 5 6 7

1   3 4   6   1 2 3   5   7   1 2 3 4 5 6 7   1 2   4   6

1 2 3   5   7   1 2   4   6   1   3 4   6   1 2 3 4 5 6 7

82.

1 te te 2 te 3 te   1 te 2 3   1 te te   te   te   1 te   te   te

1 te   te   te   1 te te   te   te   1 te 2 3   1 te te 2 te 3 te

1 te 2 3   1 te te   te   te   1 te te 2 te 3 te   1 te   te   te

1 te te   te   te   1 te   te   te   1 te 2 3   1 te te 2 te 3 te

41

83.

84.

85.

1 2 3 4 5 6 7 8   1   3 4 5 6 7   1 2   4 5 6 7 8   1 2   4   6

1 2   4 5 6 7 8   1   3 4 5 6 7   1 2   4   6   1 2 3 4 5 6 7 8

1   3 4 5 6 7   1 2 3 4 5 6 7 8   1 2   4   6   1 2   4 5 6 7 8

1 2   4   6   1   3 4 5 6 7   1 2 3 4 5 6 7 8   1 2   4 5 6 7 8

86.

1 te 2 te 3 te te   1   2 te   te   1 te 2   3   te   1 te   te   te

1 te   te   te   1 te 2   3   te   1   2 te   te   1 te 2 te 3 te te

1   2 te   te   1 te   te   te   1 te 2 te 3 te te   1 te 2   3   te

1 te   te   te   1 te 2   3   te   1   2 te   te   1 te 2 te 3 te te

87.

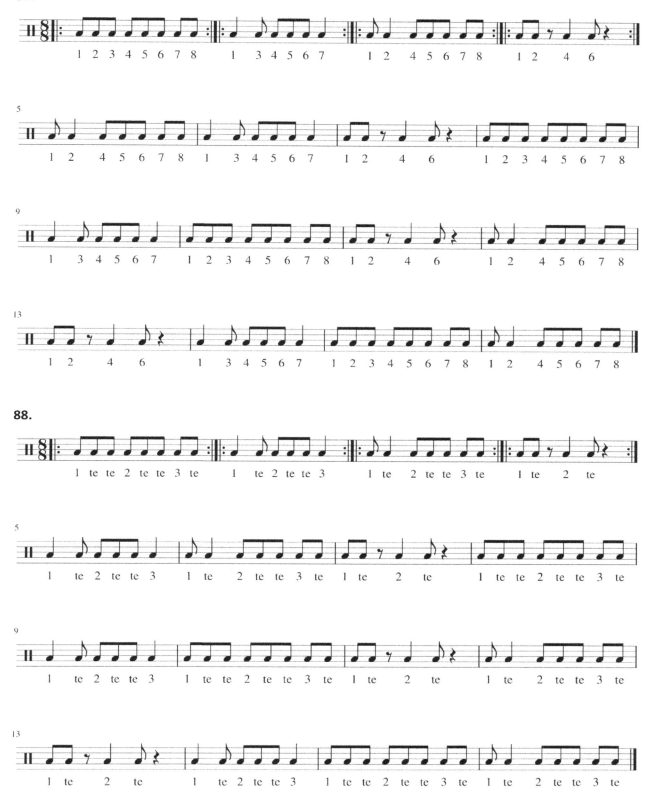

88.

91.

92.

93.

94.

95.

1   2 ta 3   4   5 ta 6   7 ta   1   3 ta 4   6   1 ta 2   3   5   7   1   2 ta   4   6

5

1   2 ta   4   6   1 ta 2   3   5   7   1   3 ta 4   6   1   2 ta 3   4   5 ta 6   7 ta

9

1   3 ta 4   6   1 ta 2   3   5   7   1   2 ta 3   4   5 ta 6   7 ta   1   2 ta   4   6

13

1 ta 2   3   5   7   1   2 ta   4   6   1   3 ta 4   6   1   2 ta 3   4   5 ta 6   7 ta

96.

1   te ta te   2   te ta 3   te ta   1   te ta 2   3   1 ta te   te   te   1   te ta   2   3

5

1   te ta   2   3   1 ta te   te   te   1   te ta 2   3   1   te ta te   2   te ta 3   te ta

9

1   te ta 2   3   1 ta te   te   te   1   te ta   2   te ta 3   te ta

12

1   te ta   2   3   1 ta te te   te   te   1 te ta   2   3   1 te ta 2 3   1 te ta te   2 te ta 3 te ta

97.

1 2 ta 1 2 3 ta 1 2 ta 1 1 ta 2 1 1 ta 2 1 3 2 1 2 ta 2 1

1 2 ta 2 1 1 ta 2 1 3 2 1 1 ta 2 1 1 2 ta 1 2 3 ta 1 2 ta

1 1 ta 2 1 1 ta 2 1 3 2 1 2 ta 1 2 3 ta 1 2 ta 1 2 ta 2 1

1 ta 2 1 3 2 1 2 ta 2 1 1 1 ta 2 1 1 2 ta 1 2 3 ta 1 2 ta

98.

1 te ta 2 te 3 ta te te ta 1 2 ta te (3) te 1 ta te 2 3 te 1 te ta 2 3

1 te ta 2 3 1 ta te 2 3 te 1 2 ta te (3) te 1 te ta 2 te 3 ta te te ta

1 2 ta te (3) te 1 ta te 2 3 te 1 te ta 2 te 3 ta te te ta

1 te ta 2 3 1 ta te 2 3 te 1 te ta 2 3 1 2 ta te (3) te 1 te ta 2 te 3 ta te te ta

LESSON 10 - SEXTUPLETS

99.

100.

101.

102.

107.

108.

LESSON 11 – QUINTUPLETS AND SEPTUPLETS

109.

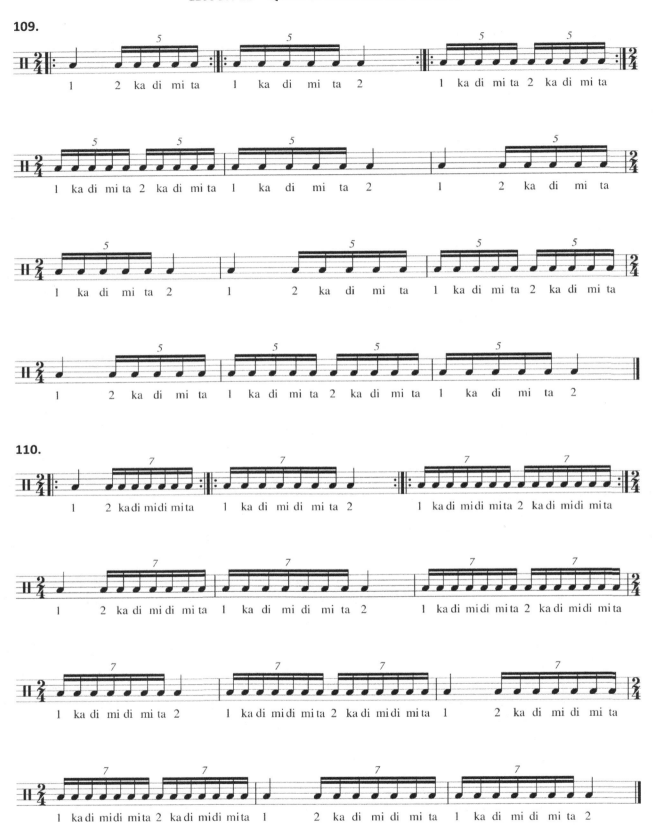

110.

111.

112.

113.

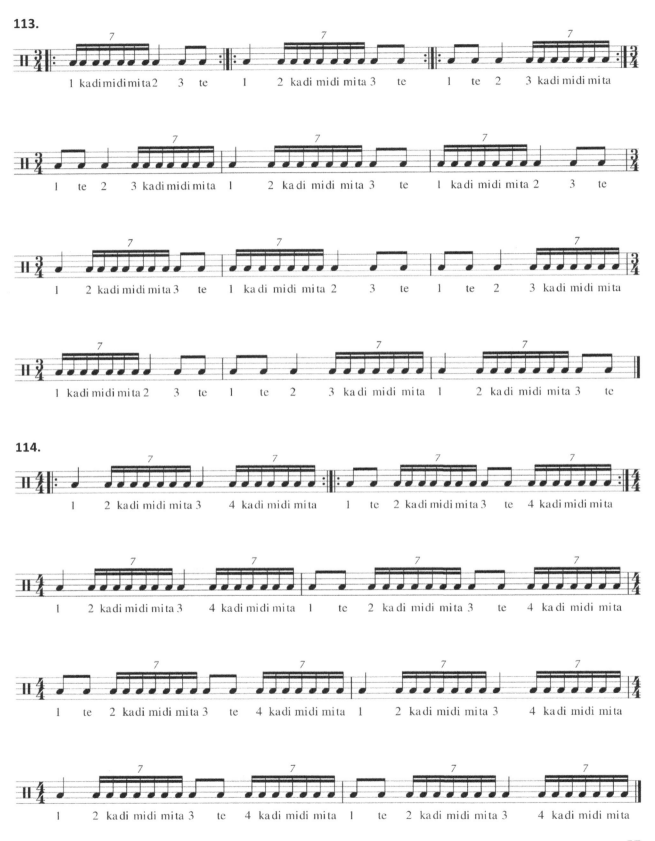

114.

115.

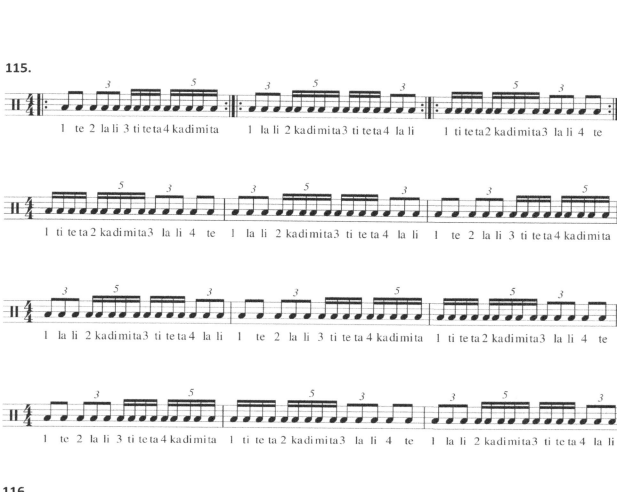

116.

LESSON 12 – ASYMMETRICAL MEASURES II

117.

118.

119.

120.

121.

122.

61

125.

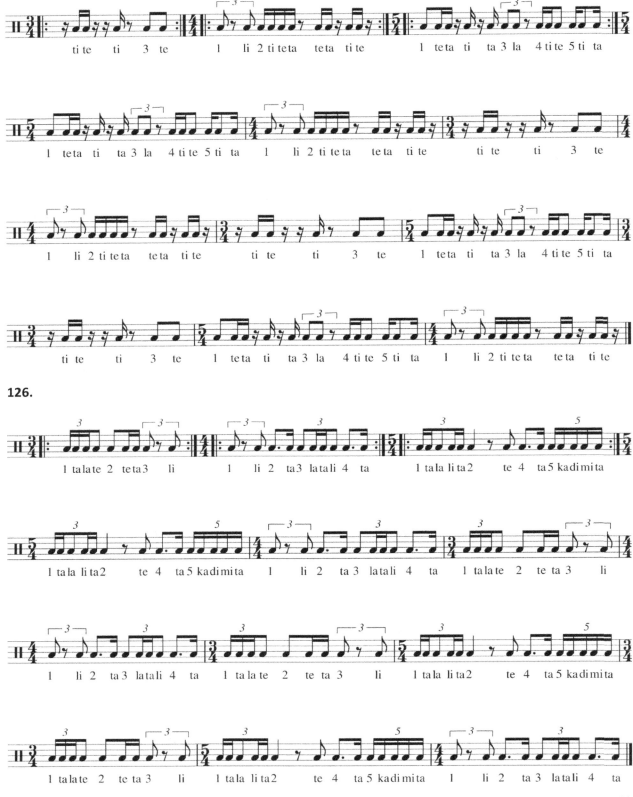

126.

127.

128.

129.

130.

131.

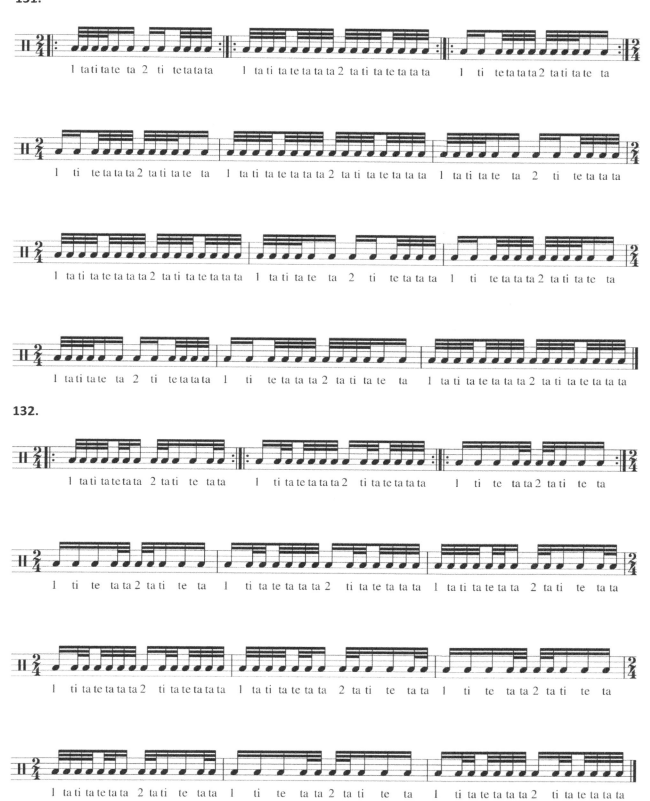

132.

LESSON 14 – HALF NOTE GETS THE BEAT

133.

134.

135.

136.

137.

138.

137.

1 te ta 2 ti ta ti ta ti ta 3 te ta 1 2 te ta la li
1 2 te ta la li ti ta 3 te ta 1 te ta 2 ti ta ti ta
ti ta 3 te ta 1 te ta 2 ti ta ti ta 1 2 te ta la li
1 te ta 2 ti ta ti ta 1 2 te ta la li ti ta 3 te ta

138.

1 ti ta ti te 3 te ta 1 ti te 2 te ta ti ta 1 la li 2 li 3 ti te ta
1 la li 2 li 3 ti te ta 1 ti te 2 te ta ti ta 1 ti ta ti te 3 te ta
1 ti te 2 te ta ti ta 1 ti ta ti te 3 te ta 1 la li 2 li 3 ti te ta
1 ti ta ti te 3 te ta 1 la li 2 li 3 ti te ta 1 ti te 2 te ta ti ta

139.

140.

LESSON 15 – POLYRHYTHMS

Below are a number of common polyrhythms written in several different manners. It should be noted that counting polyrhythms is simply a matter of finding the lowest common denominator and dividing that number by the multiple of the two contrasting rhythms. We will begin by looking at the polyrhythm two-over-three. The lowest common denominator of these two numbers is six. Since three goes into six twice and two goes into six three times, the polyrhythm can be counted as seen below (all notes in parenthesis are not played).

2-over-3

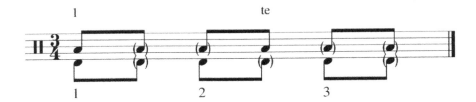

Several different ways of expressing the same example are notaed blow.

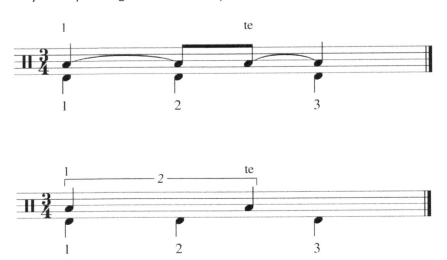

Two-over-three and three-over-two will ultimately sound the same, but they are felt differently. Six is still the common deominator however, the underlying subdivision chages as seen below.

3-over-2

Several different ways of expressing the 3-over-2 are notated blow.

The following examples follow the procedures set above (the common denominator of three and four is twelve – three goes into twelve four times and four goes into twelve three times).

3-over-4

4-over-3

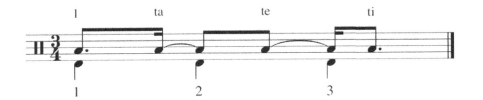

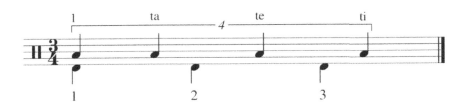

2-over-5

5-over-2

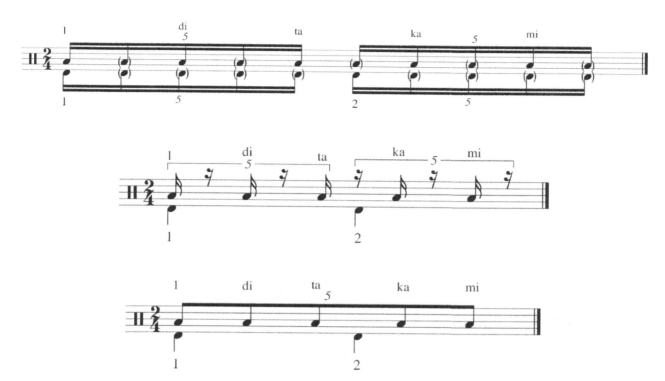

5-over-3

3-over-5

4-over-5

5-over-4

Made in the USA
Coppell, TX
03 March 2024